Some of the leaflets helped. Some REALLY didn't! Besides, I like to find things out for myself. When we got home, the first thing I did was search 'what is autism'. I kind of wish I hadn't, though.

Most of the answers I got sound really

COMPLICATED,
and sometimes really SCARY.

I printed out a few of them. (I'll show you later!)

I couldn't just ACCEPT them. I had to EXPLORE them!

That's why I've decided to write this journal: it will be a record of my Official Autism Project about what 'autistic' really means — well, what it means to ME.

I'm going to find out whatever I can during each week and write about it here every Sunday.

LET AUD'S OFFICIAL AUTISM PROJECT BEGIN!

Week 1

WHAT'S A SPECTRUM?

I want to explore one of my COMPLICATED and SCARY search results straight away. It used a phrase I don't quite understand. This is it:

> Autism, or autism spectrum disorder, can take multiple forms.

First, I want to understand just three words of it:

AUTISM — The condition I've got

SPECTRUM — ??

DISORDER — Something that's going wrong? Is that really true? I'll need to think about this!

We've learned a bit about spectrums in science at school. It didn't seem very useful at first, though!

Colour spectrum

A colour spectrum shows all the different colours of light humans can see. It's a bit like a rainbow. Instead of looking like stripes, the colours fade and blur into each other. You can find all sorts of colours, if you look for them.

> I'm going to stick a picture of a colour spectrum to the back of this book!

CONTENTS

AUD'S OFFICIAL AUTISM PROJECT 2

WEEK 1: What's a spectrum? 4

WEEK 2: How do people react? 8

WEEK 3: Can I trust the words? 14

WEEK 4: Can I trust the numbers?! 18

WEEK 5: Is it boys vs girls?! 22

WEEK 6: Can my label help me? 28

WEEK 7: Can I be myself? 31

WEEK 8: When should I ask for help? 37

WEEK 9: Am I the puzzle or the puzzle piece? 42

WEEK 10: How can we make life easier? 45

WHAT DOES AUTISM MEAN TO ME? 52

Glossary 54

Index 55

AUD'S OFFICIAL AUTISM PROJECT

This is the journal of ME, Audrey Goldstein, aged 10 years, 3 months and 22 days.

Today, I took a strange kind of test (which was fun). Afterwards, I was told that I am 'autistic' (which is ... confusing). It feels REALLY strange to be given a label and not know what it means!

Here's a little bit about me:

NAME: Audrey Goldstein ('Aud' for short!)
AGE: 10.31507 years
HOME: Brighton, UK
FAMILY: Me, Mum, Dad and Hummus (who's a cat)
BEST FRIEND(S): Nate Nnadi (and Hummus)
LIKES: Numbers, peanut butter, manga comics and SESQUIPEDALIAN words (LONG words!)
DISLIKES: Swimming, feathers, dogs and **ambiguity**

Of course, Mum, Dad and Dr Yun (the **psychologist** who did my test) did explain SOME things about what autism is. Dr Yun handed me a few leaflets.

Then I started thinking more about it. The fact that ALL SORTS of different colours are somewhere on a spectrum shows that autism can affect people in all sorts of different ways.

It seems quite nice to think about my autistic behaviours — all my **traits** — as colours somewhere on the spectrum.

★ Aud's Autism Example! ★

These are two of my autistic traits — I could imagine them as different colours!

☆ Often, I focus so much on what I'm doing that I forget everything else. This is GREAT for getting homework done. Dr Yun called it 'hyperfocus'. (I think this trait feels like a bright green colour!)

☆ I can find it hard to work out when people aren't talking **literally**. Sometimes, I don't realise when they're joking. (This one feels navy blue.)

GREAT TRAITS

Of course, anyone can concentrate hard or not get jokes (or both!).

Dr Yun said some people get a **diagnosis** of autism because they have SEVERAL behaviours that are common in autistic people, in particular combinations.

Writing down examples of my autistic behaviours felt helpful to me. It's interesting finding out that some of the things I do and think are common for autistic people!

These are some of my traits. Some parts of them are GREAT. Some are NOT GREAT.

TRAIT	HOW IT'S GREAT	HOW IT'S NOT GREAT
Having hyperfocus	I can concentrate hard on homework and other projects.	I forget to drink water and don't notice when I'm cold!
Being literal	I'm really precise, accurate and honest.	I don't always get people's jokes. Also, apparently, it's possible to be TOO honest.

TRAIT	HOW IT'S GREAT	HOW IT'S NOT GREAT
Being **logical**	I can spot patterns. That means I can sometimes work out what is likely to happen next.	I get confused about what people say if it doesn't follow a pattern or match up with other things they say.
Preferring a routine	I can keep up my good habits and be reliable (usually!).	I get stressed when things have to change.
Getting overwhelmed	It isn't great at all. :(	Parties can be hard because of the lights, noise and crowds of people. People think I'm being moody.
Being interesting!	My friends say my unusual way of seeing things helps **THEM** to see a different side of things.	It's completely great! :)

I think these tables are going to come in really handy! I can use this information LOGICALLY (hooray!). Maybe I can spot patterns in how I'll react in different situations. I can plan how to be more comfortable.

It might even help me work out how other people could react!!

Week 2

HOW <u>DO</u> PEOPLE REACT?

This week, my mum and I went to talk to my teachers about my diagnosis. I also told quite a lot of other people about it, when they asked how I was.

* Aud's Autism Example! *

Do people really want an honest answer when they say 'How are you?' I've noticed they sometimes raise their eyebrows when I describe having an itchy elbow or give details about how much I enjoyed lunch.

Maybe I should think about not taking it literally. That seems odd to me, though. Why would they ask if they don't want to know?

When I talked about my autism, people's reactions were very different and very surprising.

Mrs Singh-Wilson (our next-door neighbour) got a very serious look on her face, like someone had **DIED**. She started talking to me much ... more ... slowly ... and ... clearly. It was pretty weird because she's known me for ages.

Mr Henderson (my class teacher) looked a bit nervous and confused. He said he'd get back to Mum about what to do, and then he left the room **VERY** quickly.

Ms Francis (the head teacher) was really friendly — MUCH friendlier than usual, as I'm often in trouble when I go to see her! (It's usually for stuff like interrupting Mr Henderson or distracting people when I'm frustrated. Oops.)

She said she was glad we'd let her know, and that she was sure she could work with me to help me be 'more productive' at school. (Maybe she meant 'better behaved'!)

My best friend Nate's reaction was the most important to me, so I was a bit nervous when I told him. Of course I shouldn't have worried.

Nate just grinned and asked if I thought it changed anything for us. I said OBVIOUSLY not, and I told him all about the useful tables I wrote.

'Finally,' he said, 'we know why you don't die laughing at all my jokes.' Then he said HE'D just had a diagnosis too: a diagnosis that he was hilarious. There was no way I could take THAT literally!

The person whose reaction surprised me most is Leanne, who's in our class. She looked really cross, and said she didn't believe me.

That was upsetting and I didn't know what to do, so I asked Dad when I got home. We decided I should just ask her why she was angry.

I did that the next day — and I'm glad I did, because I learned a lot. Leanne said her brother's autistic, and that it means he can't live his life like we do.

Leanne and I had a really good talk then, about lots of things including the spectrum. She was really happy I understood it. We talked about how autism has a gradient as well as a spectrum, and how people get them confused.

The spectrum represents different WAYS autism can affect people. A gradient represents how MUCH it affects them.

Gradient

A gradient is a way of showing how intense or powerful something is.

This picture shows a gradient of greyness. On the left, the grey is intense and dark. It becomes lighter and less intense, until there's no grey left.

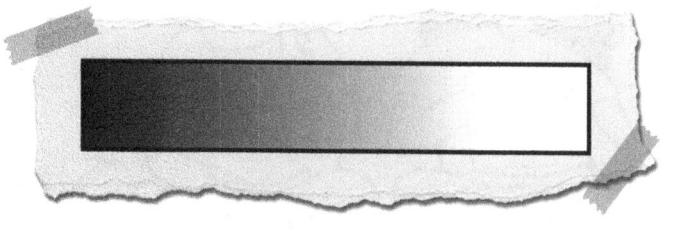

This reminded me of another one of those COMPLICATED search results I found at the very start of this project. It said this:

> Autism is a range of conditions affecting brain development that can vary from mild to **severe**.

Leanne's brother's autism is at a 'severe' point on the gradient. Mine's far less intense.

At the end of our talk, Leanne said I was right to write this journal about what autism means just to ME. I can't completely understand what it means to her or her brother, but it's important to try.

That's why I asked Leanne to write a page for this journal. I've stuck it onto the next page.

Leanne

My brother Nicky has autism. It limits his life a lot. He has trouble talking, making eye contact and sometimes using his hands. He does not go to school.

Our parents take turns looking after him at home and taking him to therapy. Therapy has helped him to control his movements. Now he can get dressed on his own and use a games controller.

We do not take Nicky into town if we can help it. The lights and noises are too hard for him. He has **meltdowns** and people think he is just having tantrums. Noise-cancelling headphones can help him, but then we cannot talk to him.

Nicky is much more relaxed at home. He can focus on a video game or watch films he knows well. They are usually cartoon films. I think he likes how exaggerated the characters are.

The best moments I have with Nicky are when he repeats sentences from his films. We were very surprised when he started doing it.

Often what he says makes sense with what we are saying. It feels like a real conversation. It shows me that my brother is funny and kind.

People are often nervous of asking me about Nicky's disability. I'm glad you asked. Aud.

I'm really glad I did, too.

> Week 3

CAN I TRUST THE WORDS?

I've thought a lot about how Leanne first reacted. Maybe she thought it wasn't fair for me to take 'autistic' as a label for myself. For her, 'autistic' means something really specific — and she called it a disability.

I looked back at another of the SCARY search results I found before I started this journal:

> Autism is a disorder that often leads to <u>limited or repetitive patterns</u> of thought and behaviour.

That sounds a lot like what Leanne said about Nicky liking to rewatch movies and repeat words from them.

It doesn't feel like that's how autism affects me, though. I think the word 'autism' is too ambiguous. I HATE ambiguity!!

This week, I've worked on finding more words for talking about my autism. It wasn't as easy as I expected, though!

There are SO MANY points of view about how to talk about autistic people. These are some things I found out:

☆ Sometimes, people who can live more easily in **society** are called 'high functioning'.

☆ Autistic people who are 'high functioning' used to be told they had 'Asperger's Syndrome'. That's because a researcher called Hans Asperger studied how some autistic people became successful (in his opinion!!).

HANS ASPERGER

☆ Lots of people still prefer the term 'Asperger's Syndrome' because that's what they've known all their lives. It's part of their identity. I REALLY get that.

☆ Lots of people choose to use that term so they can be more specific about how their autism affects them. It can tell people they're high functioning.

Then I started to read about why experts STOPPED using 'Asperger's Syndrome' as a diagnosis:

 It can suggest there's a big divide between severely autistic people and 'high-functioning' autistic people, rather than there being a gradient.

 The history's pretty upsetting: some psychologists (including Asperger himself?!) **discriminated** horribly against autistic children who didn't have a diagnosis of 'Asperger's Syndrome'.

This is all REALLY confusing! I can see both sides. I want to be accurate and specific (some of my autistic traits!). I did find out that some people have adapted the term 'Asperger's' to make it more their own, too: they call themselves 'Aspies'. I do quite like that.

I also believe in the gradient, though — and I don't want to cut myself off from people like Nicky. I know my life's really different from Nicky's, but I've spotted something.

Leanne said 'The lights and noises are too hard for him. He has meltdowns and people think he is just having tantrums.'

In my table, I wrote 'Parties can be hard because of the lights, noise and crowds of people. People think I'm being moody.'

That's not a huge divide at all.

☆ ☆ ☆ ☆ ☆ ☆ ☆ ☆ ☆

There's just **ONE** decision I've made.

Some people say we 'have autism'. Others say we 'are autistic'. To me, 'having' autism makes it sound like having flu or having a broken leg.

I don't feel like that — autism feels like part of who I am. It's part of who I've always been, even though I didn't have a word for it.

Apparently it's just tricky working out what the right word is!!

For now at least, I shall say:

Week 4

CAN I TRUST THE NUMBERS ?!

The language was interesting, but not very clear!

I always look at numbers when I feel confused like this. Maths might be hard sometimes, but numbers are never ambiguous. It's SO comforting.

This week, I decided I needed to look up some **statistics** about autism.

☁ ☆ ♡ ☆ I made diagrams! ☁ ☆ ♡ ☆

First, I looked for things that reflect MY experiences.

LIFE AT SCHOOL

In 2021, a survey found that only three in every ten autistic children in the UK were at schools that specialise in autism.

Mine isn't a specialist school.

Seven out of ten autistic children in non-specialist schools believed their lives could be better if teachers knew more about autism. More than nine out of ten thought other students didn't know enough about autism.

I totally agree!!

GETTING DIAGNOSED

Getting an autism diagnosis can take a long time. First, your doctor has to arrange for you to see an autism specialist. In the UK, the aim is that people shouldn't have to wait more than three months before seeing a specialist.

In 2022, though, most people were waiting far longer than that. Some people had been on waiting lists for YEARS!

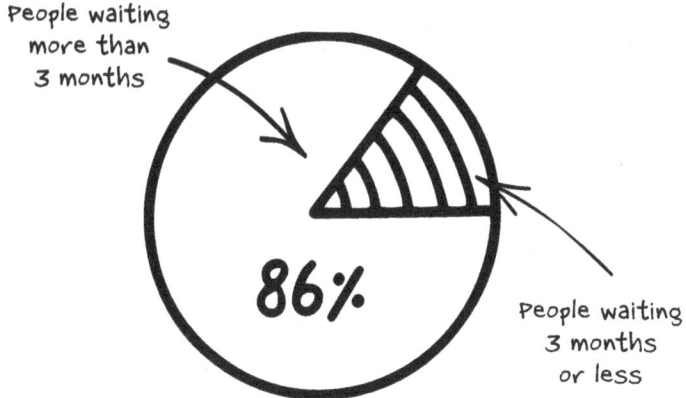

People waiting more than 3 months

86%

People waiting 3 months or less

I was **REALLY** lucky. I saw Dr Yun ten weeks after we asked my GP.

Next, I started looking at statistics about the bigger picture ...

HOW MANY PEOPLE ARE AUTISTIC?

Most articles I read said that, in 2023 in the UK, a bit over 1 in 100 people were diagnosed as being autistic. That seemed fairly straightforward to me.

Then I found a report from 2021 about how many people got autism diagnoses in the last 25 years. The number of autistic people in the UK seems to have grown a LOT.

Imagine a big school with 2,000 students. Now imagine the students represent everyone in the UK.

⭐ In 1998, reports said just one of those students would probably be autistic.

⭐ In 2008, new reports said it'd be between four and five of them.

⭐ 2018 reports said it'd be between 13 and 14.

This diagram shows how DRAMATICALLY the number's risen.

The 2023 reports meant it'd probably be 20 people out of those 2,000!

This is even stranger: in 2023, FOUR TIMES more boys than girls were diagnosed with autism.

I haven't found the numbers comforting after all.
I have SO MANY QUESTIONS.

> **The numbers suggest that more people have autism now, but ...**
> - is there more autism **awareness**?
> - are more people being tested?
> - are the tests different?

> **Apparently, autism is WAY more common in boys, but ...**
> - is it just spotted and tested more often?
> - are boys' autistic traits more noticeable?

I think I might have found a focus for next week ...

Week 5
IS IT BOYS VS GIRLS ?!

The questions I asked myself last week keep bothering me. I don't think I'll be able to answer all of them. I can't track down all the autism tests for the last 25 years, after all!

There IS a question I think I could try to explore, though:

Are boys' autistic traits more noticeable than girls'?

There's a problem with that straight away, obviously. The question kind of suggests that all boys are alike, and all girls are alike — which clearly they're not!

I'm probably going to have to go along a BIT with some **generalisations** people make about boys and girls — but usually I REALLY don't think that's helpful. I've tried to look at some of the more sciencey differences.

Let's start with stuff about everyone's brains. Apparently, different sides of the brain deal with different kinds of things.

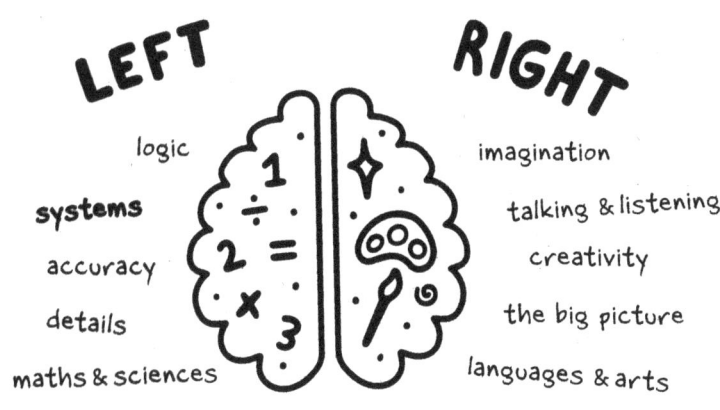

LEFT
- logic
- **systems**
- accuracy
- details
- maths & sciences

RIGHT
- imagination
- talking & listening
- creativity
- the big picture
- languages & arts

Then I looked at what some experts say about differences between the brains of people who are born as girls and people who are born as boys.

> ♂ Boys develop the left side more quickly than girls, leading to more-developed logical, problem-solving and mathematical skills.

> ♀ Girls develop the right side more quickly than boys, leading to more-developed language skills, emotions and memories.

Of course LOADS of girls are great at maths and LOADS of boys are super arty... but I suppose I have to stick with it for now. 😕

It's not too tricky to spot which of those groups of skills is similar to common autistic traits, is it?!

All this means:

⭐ many psychologists already think boys have more left-brain traits and fewer right-brain traits

⭐ left-brain traits are similar to common autistic traits, and right-brain traits are similar to things many autistic people find harder.

That left me with some questions:

? How can experts tell the difference between typical left-brain traits and autism?

? If a boy's autism is about as severe as mine, how could they tell if he's autistic — or just a boy?!

Dad helped me understand one explanation. What he did sounds pretty odd, but bear with me: he made me two cups of tea. (I DID say bear with me!)

THE TEA DEMONSTRATION

What we used:

Teaspoon

Tea 1: A cup of tea with 1 spoon of sugar in it

Tea 2: A cup of tea with 2 spoons of sugar in it

Dad told me to think about the sugar as common autistic traits that are also (apparently) common male traits: stuff like being logical and focusing on detail. That meant Tea 2 could represent a brain with a left side that's more developed: apparently, a boy's brain.

What we did:

1. Dad asked me to taste the teas. Both were pretty nice. (I usually have tea with two sugars, so Tea 2 was my favourite.)
2. Dad put two more spoons of sugar into each tea, to represent more common autistic/male traits.
3. He asked me to try the teas again.

This is what I noticed:

☆ Tea 1 (3 sugars) was a bit sweeter than I usually have ... but not extreme.

☆ Tea 2 (4 sugars) tasted EXTREMELY sweet!

I did get the point. (Well done, Dad!) I can think about it like a sum:

All of this means that, if girls have fewer noticeable left-brain traits, their common autistic traits might be harder to spot.

That might be **ONE** reason why more boys get autism diagnoses — even if the numbers of autistic boys and girls are the same. It does make sense.

However, there's something else that makes even **MORE** sense to me — because it's part of my experience. It's called 'masking'.

Masking

Masking is hiding or controlling autistic behaviours so you can fit in. It could include:
- ☆ pretending crowds aren't a problem
- ☆ practising 'normal' ways to answer questions
- ☆ trying to copy people's body language and facial expressions.

* Aud's Autism Example! *

Well ... yep. I do all that stuff!

Last week, I practised this:

> SOMEONE: How are you?
> ME: Fine, thanks. How are you?

(Apparently that's the normal way to answer!)

Autism researchers seem to agree girls are FAR more likely to mask than boys.

> Apparently, girls often learn to mask at around age 6 to 7. However, lots of people aren't tested for autism until they're 8 or older.
>
> I wonder if that's led to some misleading results: by the time the tests were taken, girls were masking their autistic traits.

None of the studies claims to know for SURE why girls mask more, but these are two ideas:

A: Girls find it easier to understand social situations, listen and choose the right words.

> These look like right-brain skills. (I'm not really convinced by this, though!)

B: There's more pressure on girls to fit in.

> This is so sad! It's even sadder that I think it's true. People always expecting girls to have more 'right-brain' skills does **NOT** help!

Week 6

CAN MY LABEL HELP ME?

I didn't end last week on a very positive note, did I?! This week's MUCH more fun.

On Tuesday evening, Mum and I had our appointment to talk to my head teacher, Ms Francis. Over the weekend, I'd filled in a kind of form about things I found challenging at school and ways I thought we could solve them. Then, during our meeting, we talked about what we could REALISTICALLY do.

It was really good. Ms Francis actually seemed a bit excited about thinking creatively. (I was quite excited, too!)

This is a summary of the most important things we said to form The Plan.

The problem	My suggestion	The plan
Sometimes the playground gets really crowded. It makes me feel anxious and panicky.	Can I come inside and use the school library at break if I want? It's quiet there.	Ms Francis wanted to let me, but the librarian, Mr Badejo, isn't in every day and I need **supervision**. However, she said she'll ask our teaching assistant if he'll go with me if things get REALLY bad.
When the classroom's noisy, I can't block out the voices to do my work. (I behave quite badly then to distract myself!)	I want to listen to calm music on my headphones, to drown out the noises.	I can't listen to music in class as it might stop me paying attention. I can try **in-ear filters**, and sit at the back where it's quieter. I can also use the library for solo work — if Mr Badejo's in.
I don't work well in a group and I don't really understand how to share tasks.	I'd rather work on my own or get different instructions for exactly which parts of group work I should do.	Mum says I should practise group work — but (if we behave) I'm allowed to be in Nate's group! He understands how I think and can kind of 'translate' all the different ideas for me. That's MUCH better than my idea!

We're going to try out The Plan next week. I think the staff must have talked about it on Wednesday, though, because two really nice things happened.

Mrs Woodley (our school caretaker) came to find me at break. She said her niece is autistic too, and she asked if she could talk to me about it at some point. I said yes. It felt good that she asked.

Mr Henderson asked me to stay behind for a minute at the end of class. I was CERTAIN I was in trouble again, but he said he'd done some reading about autism and he thinks The Plan looks good.

He said I can do excellent work when I focus, and that he's looking forward to seeing it.

I said, 'Me too'. 😊

CAN I BE MYSELF?

I messed up this week. I REALLY messed up.

Let's rewind. When I went to school on Monday, I felt great. I was looking forward to starting The Plan.

I felt like The Plan would flip a switch that meant everyone would have to see things my way for once, rather than the other way around. I didn't have to do things their way any more.

This is what I thought:

That may sound GREAT in theory. In practice, it really wasn't.

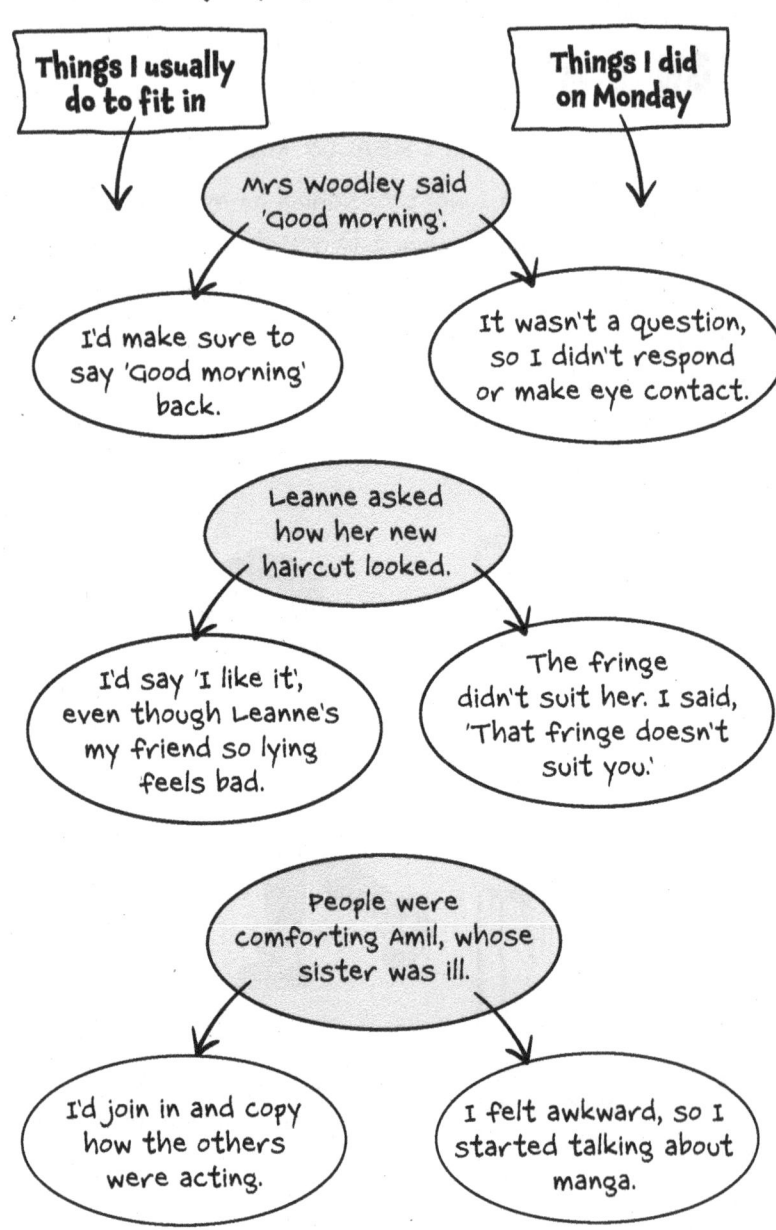

> When I finished my maths work quickly, Mr Henderson said, 'Kaye looks like she needs some help with hers.'

> I don't know – this hasn't happened before!

> I said, 'Yes, she's really slow. Ms Francis said you have to let me read.' Then I went off to the library.

Then:

☆ I told a teaching assistant he should stop helping other people and supervise me.

☆ I didn't go to PE because it's always noisy.

Finally:

> Do you want to come over after school and play Utopia 4?

> No, I don't. I don't want to pretend to enjoy that silly game any more.

Nate just looked at me hard and walked away. I felt a bit confused.

At the end of the day, I was **NOWHERE NEAR** as exhausted as usual. Ms Francis called my parents into school, though. Then the drive home was nearly silent.

I turned everything over and over in my head. I was in trouble. It looked like The Plan was in danger. Even Nate had turned his back on me.

Apparently I'd caused ALL THAT by reacting in a logical, honest way. I WAS JUST BEING MYSELF.

If that had got me in trouble, I didn't feel sad or sorry.

I felt ANGRY.

When we got home, Dad said we had to Have A Talk. (I've learned that's different from 'talking'.)

Mum started, 'Aud, we're disappointed in you — but we're not angry.' It was as though the word uncorked all the things I was feeling.

'Well I'M angry!!' I exploded. Hot tears were escaping.

> You told me lying is wrong, but I get in trouble for telling the truth!

> You told me I didn't have to hide what I thought, but now telling people is wrong!

> You told me not understanding people wasn't my fault, but I'm being punished for it!

Dad looked like he was about to shout back, but he took a deep breath.

Mum had gone a bit pale, but her voice was steady.

The Start of 'The Talk'

Mum: Do you understand that you upset a lot of people today, Aud?

(I looked confused.)

Mum: You didn't know? Well, you hurt people's feelings.

Me: Are their feelings more important than mine?!

Dad: No — but they're still important.

Mum: What was it today that changed? Why did you suddenly stop liking people?

Me: I didn't! It's exhausting wearing a mask ALL THE TIME! If THEY didn't like ME today, maybe they never liked the real me anyway!

Mum and Dad went a bit quiet after I said that. They asked if I really felt like I was wearing a mask.

As my answer, I showed them all the information I'd found on masking. Then I did my maths homework to calm myself down.

Later, Mum came to tell me they were impressed by my research. She asked if I'd rather do some more reading instead of having another Talk.

> Thank you, Mum, for letting me choose this!

She suggested I look up what a 'social filter' is.

Social filter

Using a 'social filter' in their minds is how people make their responses suitable in society. It's how they decide which thoughts they say or show to the world, and which they keep to themselves.

So ... does that mean that EVERYONE has to filter themselves a bit? Is masking just a super-extreme version of that? Maybe being myself doesn't just have an on/off switch.

Maybe I need some help to work it out properly, though.

Week 8

WHEN SHOULD I ASK FOR HELP?

Until now, Aud's Official Autism Project has been pretty much a solo effort — although I thank Dad for the Tea Demonstration!

Last week, though, I learned something important. Sometimes, I just don't know what questions I should be asking. (After all, I wouldn't have thought of researching social filters if Mum hadn't suggested it!)

To try to put right the things I did last week, I need some help.

First, I wanted to do more research following Mum's suggestion. There were more details about social filters.

> People can learn how to filter, but the skill is closely linked to the development of empathy in children.

Empathy

Empathy is the ability to:
1. understand the feelings of other people
2. share and/or respect those feelings.

Lots of people think autistic people don't have empathy. Some even believe we don't feel emotions at all!! (Reading that really shocked me.)

I CAN share and respect feelings. I just have trouble understanding what they are, unless I'm told.

* Aud's Autism Example! *

Last week proved I can't always work out when people want honesty, because I find it so hard to read their facial expressions and other clues. That's why I upset Leanne by telling her what I thought of her haircut.

I looked back at the fourth (and last!) of the SCARY search results I printed out before I started this journal:

> People with autism spectrum disorder can find it difficult to communicate and form relationships.

I DO find it difficult, but my relationships with my friends and family are important to me.

I've decided I could start by doing one or both of these things:

☆ work on reading facial expressions (Best for people I don't know well?)
☆ ask people to explain how they feel.

(Best for close relationships?)

The close relationship I really wanted to fix was with Nate. Dad suggested I apologise first, because Nate felt hurt by what I'd done. That seemed logical.

Nate said he was surprised and pleased that I apologised. He hadn't stopped liking me at all!

Then I asked him the BIG QUESTION:

❝ HOW did I hurt your feelings? ❞

This is what Nate said:

❝ When you said you didn't want to play the game with me, it sounded like you didn't want to see me at all.
I understand what you meant, now — but you called one of my interests silly. ❞

That made me realise a few things:
- ☆ People don't take everything I say literally.
- ☆ Other people's interests are special to them (like mine are to me).
- ☆ My best friend will always try to understand me. 😊

I also apologised to the other people I'd hurt (the ones on pages 32 and 33!). I asked them all that big question, too. I learned a LOT from their answers.

Leanne

❝ I couldn't change my hair, so what you said wasn't helpful — it was just hurtful and embarrassing. ❞

☆ This told me the truth isn't always VALUABLE. I could try harder to spot people's reactions after I speak, and apologise if I've got it wrong.

❝ I needed people to be kind, but you made the conversation all about you. ❞

Amil

☆ I shouldn't interrupt. I shouldn't just change a group conversation to suit me, even if I don't quite know how to join in.

Mr Henderson

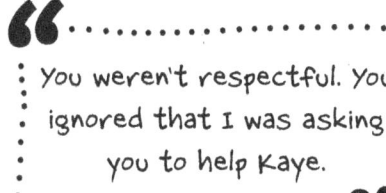
"You weren't respectful. You ignored that I was asking you to help Kaye."

 The plan doesn't mean I can do whatever I like. I didn't understand about Kaye: perhaps I could (politely!) ask Mr Henderson to give literal instructions.

Mrs Woodley

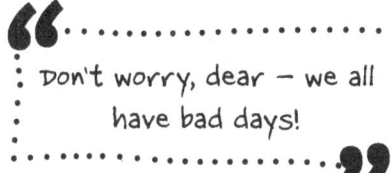
"Don't worry, dear — we all have bad days!"

I think the biggest lesson I've learned is that I can't reason everything out on my own. Some things can't be explained logically. I just have to learn and practise what to do — and ask people to help me by explaining.

Week 9

AM I THE PUZZLE OR THE PUZZLE PIECE ❓

This week, I started out by looking for advice in other places. I've found **LOADS** of stuff I can explore in the future.

There are books about living with autism that could be helpful and encouraging, some written as **autobiographies**. There are even 'handbooks' and 'survival guides' aimed at children and young adults. I'm definitely going to get some of them.

Autism charities give some helpful tips, too:

- Take breaks!
- Set a routine!
- Carry a comfort item!
- Set **boundaries** to protect yourself!
- Identify what challenges you!

I found a story about some of the charities, too. It's all about this:

A jigsaw puzzle piece is sometimes used as a symbol for autism — but not everyone likes it.

Remember the different opinions about language on pages 15 and 16? This is just as big a deal.

The jigsaw-piece symbol was used by some early autism charities.

One group said they used it to represent a puzzling condition. Another said it represented a search for answers. (I think they meant that was like searching for puzzle pieces. If it took them that long, they must have been RUBBISH at jigsaws!)

However, it looks like most people REALLY disagree with using the jigsaw symbol. Some even find it really offensive. These are some of the reasons:

☆ Jigsaws are related to children, not adults. Adults are being left out.

☆ Jigsaws are pictures that have fallen apart and need fixing.

☆ A piece on its own suggests a jigsaw's not complete: there's something missing.

I'm not sure about the first point — Dad **LOVES** massive jigsaws! The other two sound worrying, though. No one wants to think of themselves as being broken or having missing parts.

I kept reading (of course!). Some autistic people like the jigsaw-piece image:

☆ Understanding they have autism completed a puzzle for **THEM**.

☆ Jigsaw pieces make connections.

... and I've thought of a third reason why the jigsaw symbol might be good.

While I've been putting together this journal, I do feel like pieces are fitting into place. It's not like I felt broken, or like I had a big gap where bits were missing, though.

It's more like **I'M** the jigsaw piece — or I **HAVE** the piece. I'm just finding ways to fit things around it: what autism means to me, how my relationships work, the situations in which I feel comfortable and everything.

I'm finding the pieces that fit me. I don't have to change to fit them.

Week 10

HOW CAN WE MAKE LIFE EASIER?

This weekend, I completely burned out. It's not the first time it's happened, but I think it might be the worst.

Autistic burn-out

Burn-out is extreme exhaustion after too much effort. It can happen to anyone, usually after long periods of stressful work.

Autistic burn-out usually happens suddenly and intensely. It can cause meltdowns, feelings of being overwhelmed and 'shut-downs': the loss of ability to **interact**, including to speak.

The last couple of weeks have been INTENSE for my thoughts and feelings. Then things became pretty intense around me, too.

Friday was Nate's birthday. (I got him Utopia 5, as an extra way to show I respected his hobbies!)

His mum had rented the local pool for the party and pre-ordered a MOUNTAIN of pizza. We'd been excited about it for WEEKS.

I didn't imagine what it'd actually be like:

☆ There was an awful lot of movement as people splashed about.

☆ Any kind of personal space was impossible.

☆ I tried really hard to talk to everyone (especially because I was still making up for My Bad Day).

☆ Worst of all, the pool was VERY loud and VERY echoey.

I got more and more overwhelmed. It was Nate's birthday, though! Even I know you don't simply leave your best friend's party.

Nate checked on me, but I'd just learned I shouldn't ALWAYS tell the truth. This seemed like a perfect time to put that into practice.

I told Nate I was having a GREAT time.

Eventually, I spotted his mum taking steaming pizza boxes into the café and asked if I could help. She asked if I wanted to sort out the drinks in the little kitchen — on my own. I like Nate's mum.

I was quiet at home on Friday night. Mum and Dad didn't seem surprised. I went to bed really early.

Then Saturday didn't really exist. It was like my head was still full of everything that had happened the day before, and there wasn't space for me to work out anything else.

When I wasn't sleeping, I stayed in my room and read. Not more research — I just reread my old manga comics. Mum and Dad tried to be really quiet whenever they came upstairs.

This morning, I felt better. I'd also had time to think. I knew this wasn't my first burn-out — but it was the first time we could recognise it.

When Mum suggested we start thinking about ways to keep me happier and healthier, I was MORE than ready.

I knew I needed to put all my research to good use. I knew we needed to make another plan!

We decided to look back at those tips I found on the charities' sites. They kind of generalise about people's autistic traits. We thought they could be our starting points, though.

- This is related to my hyperfocus.
- I don't notice when I get cold / tired / hungry.

A: Take breaks!

- I need to rest — but other people can't always be there to remind me.

- I've LOVED this Sunday journal-writing routine.
- I have a school routine already.

B: Set a routine!

- Could I schedule particular times for particular activities?

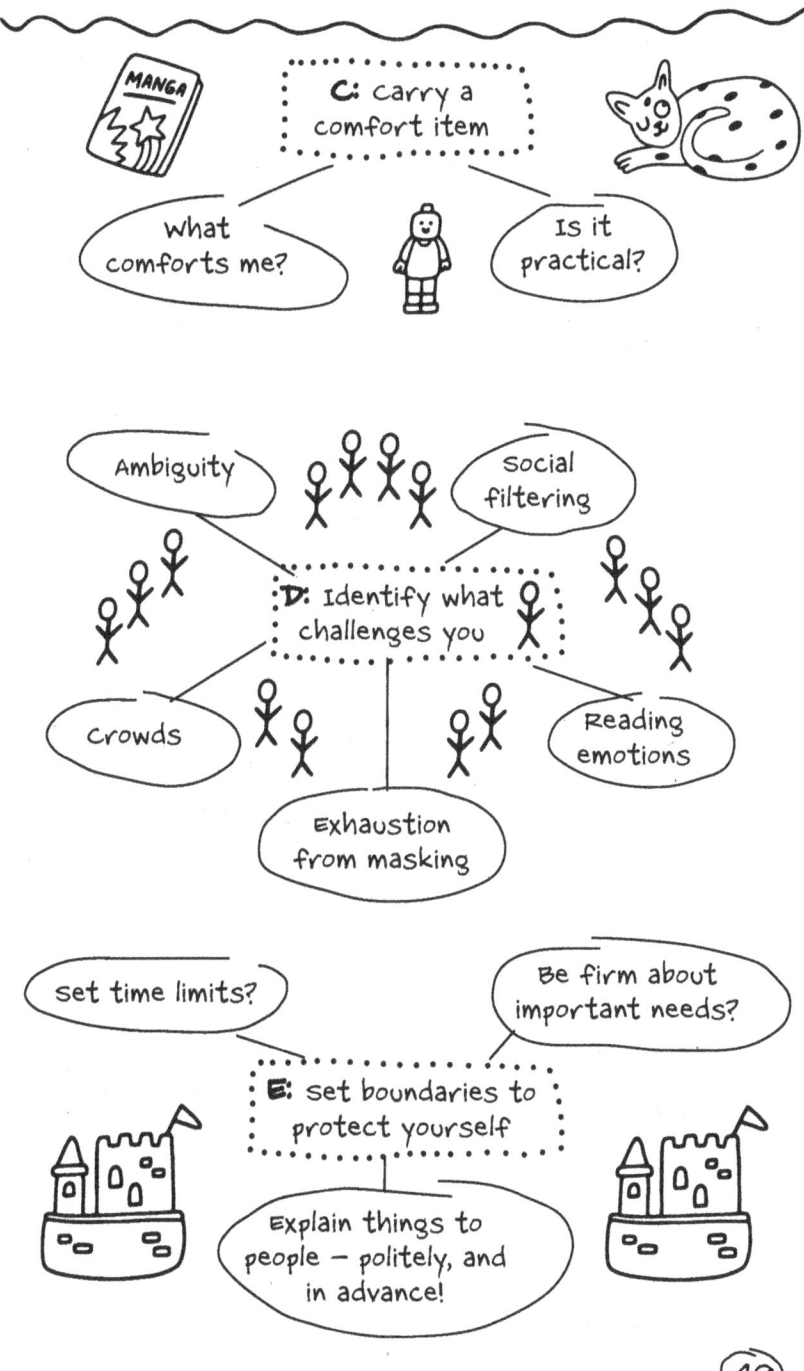

* AUD'S OFFICIAL ACTION PLAN! *

A	When I'm busy doing something, we'll set timers far enough away that I can't just turn them off. When they go off, I'll have to get up, and I'll check: • Do I need a jumper? • Shall I have a snack? • Shall I get more water? • Do I need the loo?!
B	• I'll invite Nate to my house on Thursdays, and visit him on Fridays (if he wants!). • 7pm–8:30pm every day is manga-reading time. • Saturday nights are family-game nights (when it works for Mum and Dad). • Sunday afternoons are for journal writing.
C	I'll carry manga comics. They're small and light and always calm me down.
D	Before going somewhere, we'll consider what might make me uncomfortable. ↓ I'll be prepared. ↓ I'll be on the look-out for reaching my boundaries.

E (Part 1)	If I feel nervous with someone new, I might: • choose to explain I usually take things pretty literally • consider things in my head before saying them out loud • look out for sad and hurt expressions!
E (Part 2)	We'll set time limits, be firm with them and explain them to people.

* Aud's Autism Example! *

At Nate's party, I could've been prepared to spend only 30 minutes with everyone in the pool. I'd have explained that to Nate, and made sure I could then go somewhere quiet for a while. If I felt good, I could choose to go back!

That feels like a good plan. All these things seem doable, and they should make life easier.

WHAT DOES AUTISM MEAN TO ME?

I almost can't believe how far I've come since I started Aud's Official Autism Project!

I've looked at spectrums and gradients, words and numbers, negatives and positives ... and I feel like I'm STARTING to get a grip on it all.

At least, I feel like I understand it enough that I can help myself.

Obviously, autism isn't the ONLY important thing that makes me 'me'. It's a really BIG part of me, though: it shapes how I think and how I relate to people.

I've also formed some OPINIONS. Let's take one more quick look at a few of those first SCARY search results, because I want to ARGUE with them.

> Autism, or autism spectrum <u>disorder</u>, can take multiple forms.

> Autism is a <u>disorder</u> that often leads to limited or repetitive patterns of thought and behaviour.

> People with autism spectrum <u>disorder</u> can find it difficult to communicate and form relationships.

Those writers might be experts — but I really think they made a mistake about something. Autism doesn't feel like a disorder to me: it's not something that's going wrong. I think it's just a DIFFERENT order.

Autism does mean I have some challenges. It also gives me superpowers, though!

I can use my super-logic to face the challenges. I can super-reason my way through a lot of them! I can use my super-focus to explore more of the information out there — and, sometimes, use my super-literal understanding to make sense of it!

Writing all this could feel like I'm pulling things together as some sort of conclusion.

It isn't really, though: I'm an explorer just setting out.

It makes me proud to say:

I'M AN AUTISTIC EXPLORER!

Glossary

ambiguity	the idea that things could have more than one possible meaning
autobiographies	books about the authors' own experiences
awareness	knowledge and understanding
boundaries	walls (or the idea of walls) around something, marking its end or its limits
diagnosis	identification of a particular condition
discriminated	behaved badly towards a type of person because of something seen as a difference
generalisations	judgements about whole groups of people or things generally, rather than considering differences within them
in-ear filters	earplugs with holes through them that can deaden some kinds of sound and let other kinds into the ear, to reduce noises that can confuse or bother you
interact	respond to other people or things, usually also getting responses from them
literally	completely and exactly, in the most straightforward sense
logical	showing clear, sensible reasoning
psychologist	expert on how people think
severe	serious and extreme
society	group or groups of people living together, and how they behave together
statistics	information based on numbers
supervision	the process of watching over someone or something

systems things following the same rules to fit or work together as a whole

traits features or ways of behaving that are linked to a particular person

Index

Asperger's Syndrome 15–16

books 42

burn-out 45–47

charities 42–43, 48–49

colour spectrum 4–5

diagnosis 2, 6, 15–16, 19–27

empathy 37–39

facial expressions 26, 38–40, 51

gradient 11–12, 16

hyperfocus 5–6, 48, 53

left brain / right brain 23–27

masking 26–27, 31, 35–36, 49

overwhelm 7, 45–46

(The) Plan 28–31, 48–51

routine 7, 42, 48, 50

school 9, 18, 28–33, 40–41

social filter 36–37, 49

statistics 18–21

tea demonstration 24–25

Now answer the questions …

1 On page 10, what does 'hilarious' mean?

2 According to the articles Aud read, how many UK people out of 100 were diagnosed as being autistic in 2023?

3 What was Dad trying to explain using the Tea Demonstration on pages 24–25?

4 Look at pages 31–36. How do you feel about Aud's experiences in Week 7?

5 On page 33, Mr Henderson said, 'Kaye looks like she needs some help with hers.' What did he really mean?

6 On page 34, Aud uses capital letters to start the words 'Have A Talk'. What does this suggest about the conversation?

7 Reread pages 46 and 47. Describe one thing at Nate's party that made Aud feel uncomfortable, and one thing that made her feel comfortable.

8 From what you know about Aud, how do you think setting time limits might help her?